ISBN: 9781950500475

duopress books are available at special discounts when purchased in bulk for sales promotions as well as for fund-raising or educational use. Special editions can be created to specification. Contact us at hello@duopressbooks.com for more information.

Duo Press LLC.
8 Market Place, Suite 300
Baltimore, MD 21202

Distributed by Workman Publishing Company, Inc.
Published simultaneously in Canada by Thomas Allen & Son Limited.

To order: hello@duopressbooks.com
www.duopressbooks.com
www.workman.com

Manufactured in China
10 9 8 7 6 5 4 3 2 1

The Secret Powers of Animals

PLAYFUL AS A PANDA,

PEACEFUL AS A SLOTH

SASKIA LACEY • ILLUSTRATED BY ALEXANDRA BALL

dp
duopress

CONTENTS

A NOTE TO PARENTS

Our world is filled with wondrous creatures. There are brave, wise, and kindly beasts who have many lessons to teach! Wolves are inspiring examples of loyalty. Penguins, bold and tireless, are adventure experts. Polar bears embody selfless love. Sloths, nature's happy slowpokes, are marvelously skilled at taking it easy.

This book helps young ones master life's most important skills. As you read together, ask children to think about what each animal can teach them. Then, celebrate what they have learned! The activities encourage readers to get outside, connect with others, and make beautiful things with their hands.

Study these fantastic creatures closely.
We can learn from their wild wisdom!

Happy adventuring,
Saskia Lacey

PANDA

Play

For the silly panda bear cub, even walking is an adventure. The happily clumsy creature shuffles, teeters, flops, and rolls. Somersaulting might be the cub's fastest mode of travel!

Have you ever been struck with the sillies? A playful bolt of energy zips through your body, making you wiggle, spin, and leap. You long to run through the grass, dive in a pool, and roll down a hill...all at the same time.

Panda bear cubs know the feeling well. For these playful creatures, everything is a game and everyone is a friend. Cubs spend their days swinging from branches, splashing in pools, and rolling across the grass. Try being as playful as a panda today!

ROLY-POLY PANDA

Who can roll the fastest? Find out with a somersault race! Mark the start and the end of the race. Then get to rollin'.

See if you can spell out the first letter of your name using somersaults.

CUB FOR A DAY Pandas have busy schedules. So many ways to play and so little time. How many panda tasks can you fit in a day?

My Panda To-Do List
★ dangle from a branch
★ roll down a hill
★ cuddle someone
★ snore in the sun
★ splash in the water
★ frolic with a friend

DOLPHIN

Friendship

Awesome acrobats, dolphins spin, flip, dive, and leap. But their secret superpower is friendship!

Are you a chatterbox? You might have a lot in common with the dolphin. This sea creature adores talking. It "chats" using clicks, whistles, squeaks, and squawks.

Dolphins build strong friendships by spending quality time together. They learn, play, hunt, and travel in a group. Dolphins even have BFFs—Best Flipper Friends! Some dolphins stay pals for decades.

How are you like the dolphin? Would you rather spend time playing alone or with friends?

WHAT'S YOUR DOLPHIN NAME?

Every dolphin has a signature whistle. This "name" is given to the dolphin by its mother. Use whistles, clicks, or squawks to design your own dolphin name!

SQUEAK

SQUEAK

HIDE-AND-SQUEAK

Dolphins build strong friendships through play and communication. Play these games, in or out of water, to connect with friends.

Indoors: Hide an object in a room. Help your friend find the object by giving dolphin directions like the ones below.

Squeak: You're close
Squawk: Super close!
Click: Wrong way

Pool: Tell your friend to close their eyes. Then, give your friend dolphin directions about where you are in the pool. Just like Marco Polo but with more squeaks and squawks!

ECHO INVESTIGATOR

Dolphins can "see" with their ears. They use echoes to learn about their surroundings. From an echo, a dolphin can learn the size, speed, and location of an object.

ELEPHANT

Wisdom

Elephants are wise animals. They know the value of learning from the past and planning for the future.

Kind, intelligent creatures, elephants value friends and family. They protect and care for each other. If one elephant is sick, another is sure to lend a helping trunk.

Known for their keen memory, elephants can remember where to find food and water. This is helpful when the herd is on a long journey. The massive mammals also use their memory to build and improve tools, like using a leafy branch for a flyswatter or a long stick for a back scratcher.

Are you as wise as an elephant? Being wise means using what you know to help yourself and others. How can you learn from your past?

Remember When?

Break out the pens and paper! Draw an elephant with big, big ears. On one ear, write down a memory. Perhaps you went to the park last week. Or, maybe you recently helped a friend. It can be any memory. You choose! On the other ear, write what you learned from the experience. Then, draw more elephants.

Once you finish, cut out each elephant. Then, grab a bunch of paper clips. Pull apart each paper clip. You will use these clips as stands.

Tape one half of the paper clip to the back of each elephant. Then, set your new animal friends on a flat surface. Presto—a herd of life lessons! Study your elephants. Grow in wisdom. Remember, the more you learn from your past, the wiser you'll become!

Materials

* paper
* pen or pencil
* scissors
* tape
* paper clips

optional: markers or colored pencils (for elephant decorating!)

HANDS-FREE!

When it comes to elephants, it's all about the nose. Elephants use their trunks in many ways. They use them to grab food, wave fronds, spray water, and hug friends. Elephants even use their trunks as snorkels when they swim.

Try going hands-free for an afternoon. Pretend one of your legs is a long elephant trunk. What can you do with your new trunk? Try waving to a friend. Or, use your toes to pick up and throw objects. Be as creative as you can!

HONEY BADGER

Bravery

Who's the world's most courageous creature? Is it the lion? The tiger? The bear? No, no, and nope! It's a fierce little weasel: the honey badger.

Small in size, but huge in attitude, the honey badger is a brave and feisty beast. Need proof? Just look at the animal's daring diet.

Most creatures run from bees, but the sound of a buzzing hive is sweet music to the honey badger. With a gleeful pounce, the weasel slurps up its favorite snack—bee larvae. Yuck! Another favorite honey badger treat? Poisonous snakes!

When facing a dangerous predator, the badger rises to the challenge—even if the opponent is three times its size. Remember this brave weasel when you're facing a scary situation. You may be small, but like this tough little badger, you can be brave too!

GOBBLE AND GULP

If you're making dinner for a honey badger, anything will do. These weasels aren't picky. They eat everything. Fruits, berries, birds? Yep. Insects, mammals, and amphibians? Those too.

Is there a food you've been too scared to try? Channel the honey badger and gobble it down.

ACTIVATE BADGER MODE

Sometimes acting brave can make you feel brave inside. When in danger, the honey badger strikes a tough pose. It rises on its hind legs, growls, and bares its teeth.

Practice your own tough pose. Stand tall. Puff out your chest. Bare your teeth and growl! With luck, your fierce stance will make you feel as brave as a badger.

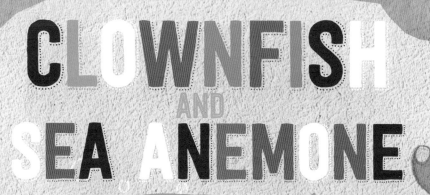

CLOWNFISH AND SEA ANEMONE

Harmony

The clownfish and sea anemone are an unlikely duo. One is a poisonous fish-eater. The other...is a fish.

When a clownfish meets a sea anemone, it dances respectfully. The fish carefully touches the anemone's poisonous tentacles. Then, after its gentle greeting, the clownfish settles in. The sea anemone will become its new home.

The secret to their strange partnership is harmony. Each creature gives the other what it needs. The sea anemone provides the clownfish with a safe home, protecting it from predators. In turn, the clownfish cleans the anemone of parasites. Together, they create a peaceful life.

Living in harmony isn't easy. Listen to others. Learn what they need. Then love them with all of your heart! You'll be as happy as a clownfish in the arms of a sea anemone.

IT TAKES TWO

Every pitcher needs a catcher, and every writer needs a reader. There are some things you can't do on your own! Another thing you can't do alone? Run a three-legged race.

Before you begin, practice walking with your partner. Listen to each other, and keep your steps in time. If you want to win, working together is a must. Otherwise, you're sure to tumble!

MATERIALS:

★ 2 markers to mark the start and end of the race (this can be anything...shoes, rope, or even stuffed animals!)

★ long fabric to tie legs together

★ timer (if you don't have enough people for a race, try to beat a timed record with your partner)

YOU AND ME UNDER THE SEA

Lights! Camera! Puppetry! Imagine life under the sea with a shoebox puppet theater. Build a colorful seascape with a friend or parent. Once your theater is in working order, it's time for the show! Act out a silly scene between a clownfish and sea anemone.

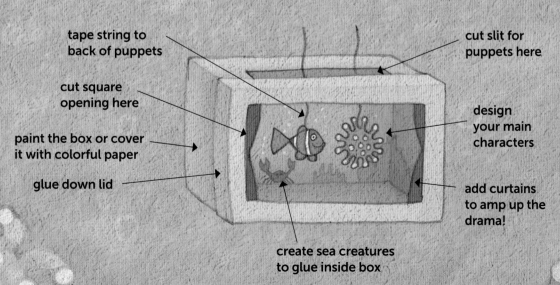

tape string to back of puppets

cut slit for puppets here

cut square opening here

design your main characters

paint the box or cover it with colorful paper

glue down lid

add curtains to amp up the drama!

create sea creatures to glue inside box

OWL

Patience

Two eyes glimmer in the pitch-black night. High in a tree, a great horned owl waits patiently. Who will be his midnight snack?

Even on the darkest night, an owl can spot its next meal scurrying through the grass. If the animal is hiding, the bird will hear its heartbeat. The owl's keen eyesight and powerful hearing make it an expert hunter, but the bird's greatest gift might be patience.

An owl can wait for hours. The bird will sit patiently on its perch until just the right moment. Then, diving silently through the air, the owl captures its prey by sneak attack. Dinner's ready!

If you want to be as patient as an owl, practice waiting. While you wait, study your surroundings. Listen and look. What do you hear? What do you see? Then, take a deep breath. Your time will come sooner than you think!

Step by Step

Making something beautiful takes time. If you want to do your best work, sometimes you have to go slow. As you complete the owl craft below, take time with each step.

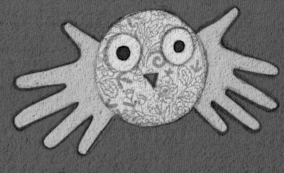

Step 1: For your owl's wings, trace two handprints.

Step 2: For your owl's body, trace something large and round, like the bottom of a big bowl.

Step 3: For your owl's eyes, trace something small and round, like the bottom of a cup. (Do this step twice.)

Step 4: For your owl's pupils, trace something tiny and round, like a quarter. (Do this step twice.)

Step 5: For your owl's beak, draw a small triangle.

Step 6: Decide what color you want each part of the owl to be. Take time to color each drawing. Then, carefully cut out each drawing.

Step 7: Glue the biggest circle onto your two handprints. Then, glue on the eyes and beak.

Step 8: Marvel at your beautiful bird!

Materials
* pencil
* paper
* colorful paper (optional)
* scissors
* glue or tape
* items to trace
* markers or colored pencils

WORTH THE WAIT

Baking is a yummy way to practice waiting. If you can make a batch of cookies without tasting the batter or peeking in the oven, you're on your way to being owl patient. Once they're ready, dig in. You've earned it!

WOLF

Loyalty

If you are a lost wolf, go ahead and howl—your loyal pack will find you. Awoooo!

Wolf packs are tight-knit families. They eat, sleep, hunt, and play together. They count on each other to survive. Wolves know the value of loyalty.

The leaders of the pack are called the alpha wolves. These are the parents. Mom and dad wolves love and care for their pups. They protect them from other animals.

Like wolves, you have a loyal pack. These are the people who love and support you. Call out to them when you are feeling lost.

Alpha in Charge
Play a game of follow the leader with your favorite packmate. Howl when they howl. Run when they run. Jump when they jump. Then, switch roles. Now, you're the alpha wolf!

REMEMBER YOUR PACK

Design a garland to pay tribute to your pack. Use colorful paper, fabric, or even pictures of wolves. On each piece of paper, write the name of a person you trust. This might be a parent, grandparent, friend, or teacher. Then, describe how this person shows loyalty. Once you are done, poke a hole in each and run the string through, then hang it in your room! Whenever you feel lost or alone, look at the garland and remember the people in your pack.

Materials
* pens or pencils
* colorful paper or fabric
* string

GIRAFFE

Gentleness

Across the savanna, a towering creature nibbles on acacia treetops. Meet Africa's gentle giant, the giraffe!

When you see a big animal, it's natural to be scared. Nature's biggest beasts are some of its most dangerous. But some big animals are kind and gentle.

The giraffe weighs thousands of pounds. It is the world's tallest animal! It is also one of the most peaceful. Even though giraffes are big and strong, they don't prey on other animals. Their diet is decidedly green: leaves, twigs, and fruit.

If you ever get the chance to feed a giraffe, there's no need to be nervous of teeth. The spotted giant will use its long tongue to gently pluck leaves from your hand.

How can you be as gentle as a giraffe?

MAKING FURRY FRIENDS

The best way to make animal friends is to treat them gently. Pet them as softly as you can. Think about how you would like to be treated if you were an animal. Soon you will have a best furry friend!

A GENTLE REMINDER

When you are feeling angry or sad, a gentle word is hard to find. Help yourself be a little kinder by making a collage of your favorite gentle things. Next time you're feeling grumpy, take time to look at your kind creation.

Materials

- ★ scissors
- ★ glue or tape
- ★ kind words and quotes
- ★ pictures of gentle creatures
- ★ favorite colors
- ★ cozy family photos

TIGER

Independence

Bengal tigers are strong and powerful. They are solitary creatures known for their independence.

Native to India, the Bengal tiger is fond of solo adventures. The big cat lives alone, marking its territory by scratching tree trunks with its long, sharp claws. At night, the tiger stalks its prey. The feline's black stripes help it blend in with its surroundings. As prey draws closer, the tiger waits patiently. Then, with a quick leap, the cat pounces!

The Bengal tiger relies on its hunting skills to survive. This big cat knows how to look after itself. This is what it means to be independent! What can you do all on your own?

FREE TO BE ME

Find a spot outdoors that you can call your own. Mark your territory clearly, using leaves, sticks, and rocks. This is your home range. Here, you make the rules. Decide where you will sleep and what you will eat. If you see an intruder, let out a fierce tiger roar!

SPOOKY SMILE

The last thing an animal wants to see is a Bengal tiger grin. The big cat has big teeth. Its canines can grow up to three inches long!

Up to the Challenge

What can you learn to do by yourself? Can you make a snack or brush your teeth? Try something new. Each skill you learn is another step toward becoming as independent as a tiger.

SLOTH

Peace

Who's that furry creature sleeping in the trees? It's the three-toed sloth! This sweet, smiling mammal knows a thing or two about peaceful living.

Sloths are all about the slow life. They climb slow. They stretch slow. They eat slooooow. It can take a month for a sloth to digest a single leaf!

Sloths live in the tropical rain forests of Central and South America. They spend most of their time in the trees, dozing the day away. Expert snoozers, sloths can sleep up to 20 hours straight!

We can learn a lot from these happy slowpokes. There's a peace that comes from taking your time, especially when it feels like the world is moving too fast. If life gets busy, think of the sloth. Slow down and watch the trees sway in the breeze. Take a nap...or three!

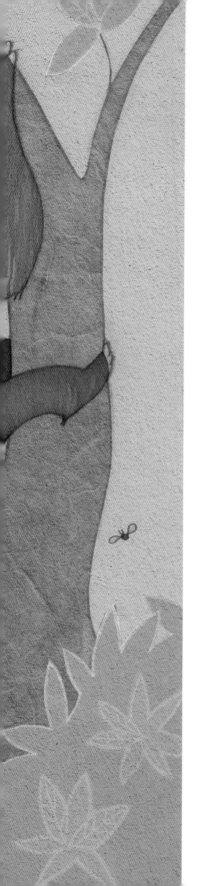

How Slow Can You Go?

Get ready for a sloth silly-off!
The game is simple. Do your very best sloth impression with a partner. The first person to laugh loses. Channel the peaceful creature by smiling, eating, and stretching in silly slow motion.

Happy Sloth Pose

Time for sloth yoga!
Picture yourself in a leafy forest. You are a sloth hanging from your favorite tree. First, lie on your back. Then, bring your knees to your chest. Hold your feet with your hands. Breathe in and out slowly.

Now, rock from side to side. You are swinging from a branch. You sway as a gentle wind blows. Breathe in and out. After a minute, let your legs drop slowly to the floor. Rest for a few moments on your back. Think happy sloth thoughts.

POLAR BEAR

LOVE

A mama polar bear loves fiercely. The Arctic is a dangerous place. Only the fiercest love will keep her babies safe.

Before her cubs are born, the mama polar bear prepares. She builds a cozy snow den. Carving the snow with her big, sharp claws, she shapes underground rooms and tunnels.

When the babies arrive, the mama bear cuddles them close. She keeps them warm. The cubs nurse happily on her milk.

For months, the new family stays underground for the long winter. As the cubs grow stronger, the mama bear grows weaker. Her cubs are well-fed, but she is starving. Still, the mama bear stays in the den to keep her babies safe. She cares for her cubs more than she does for herself!

Polar bear mamas know the meaning of love. They are warm, caring, and selfless creatures. Do you know someone who loves fiercely? How can you be more like them?

A DEN OF ONE'S OWN

Build a cozy den for someone you love! Use pillows and blankets to make the bottom of the den nice and soft. Then, drape lots of sheets over furniture. Want to take your den to the next level? Try building this one.

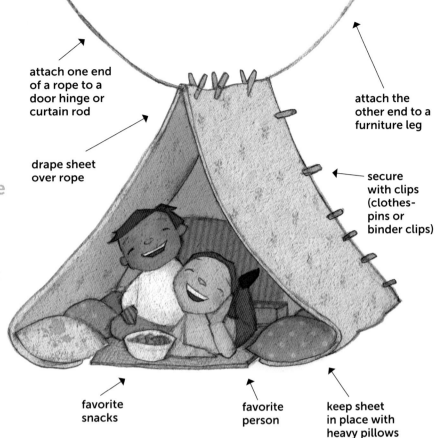

attach one end of a rope to a door hinge or curtain rod

drape sheet over rope

attach the other end to a furniture leg

secure with clips (clothes-pins or binder clips)

favorite snacks

favorite person

keep sheet in place with heavy pillows

Love like a Polar Bear

Love is kind, selfless, and brave. You can show love in many ways. Love is sharing the last slice of pizza. Love is comforting someone when they are sad. Love is a big polar bear hug!

One of the best ways to show love is by helping others. Create a "love storm" for someone who could use a little tenderness.

Draw a bunch of snowflakes. On each one, write one way you will show your love. Cut out each snowflake carefully. Then, shower someone with your love storm!

PENGUIN

Adventure

Emperor penguins aren't famous for their bravery, but they should be. Bold and tireless, these birds are always ready for adventure!

Penguins go on many exciting quests. They travel to meet their mates, hunt for food, and take care of their families. These journeys can be long and dangerous.

To look for food, emperor penguins must travel across icy terrains. They trudge through miles of snow to find water. Sometimes penguins walk more than 50 miles.

Once they reach water, penguins dive deep. They hunt for tasty fish. After they've eaten their fill, penguins set out on their next adventure—the return trip!

READY, SET, WADDLE

Who is the fastest penguin? Find out by mapping a course in your home or yard. Then it's ready, set...waddle! Shuffle as fast as you can. A few tips: Keep your feet penguin flat and your arms out to the side for balance.

ON THE HUNT

Everyone has heard of a treasure hunt, but what about an adventure hunt? Make a list of adventurous things you want to do. Your list may include cartwheels and tree climbing or fort building and bug finding. No hurry to finish the list. Great adventures take time!

My Adventure Hunt
- ★ put on a play (that I wrote!)
- ★ eat a super spicy pepper
- ★ find (and capture!) a firefly
- ★ dance under a shooting star

31

GLOSSARY

acrobat: a person who performs difficult acts for entertainment

adventure: an exciting or dangerous experience

alpha: an animal that has the most power in its group

bravery: the quality of being able to do things that are frightening; courage

communication: the act of using words, sounds, signals, or behavior to give information

design: to plan and make something

digest: to convert food into a simpler form that can be used by the body

echo: a copy of a sound that is produced by sound waves bouncing off a surface

friendship: being friends

gentleness: the quality of being kind and quiet

harmony: a pleasing combination of things; agreement

independence: freedom from outside control or support

intelligent: able to learn and understand things easily

keen: strong and sensitive; highly developed

love: a feeling of strong affection for someone

loyalty: being faithful to someone

massive: very large and heavy

patience: the ability to wait for a long time

peace: a quiet and calm state

play: (noun) activities done for fun and enjoyment

predators: animals that hunt other animals

quest: a journey

savanna: a large area of land with lots of grass and very few trees

signature: closely associated with someone or something

skill: the ability to do something through training, experience, or practice

solitary: separate from other people or animals

terrain: land of a particular kind

territory: an area that an animal uses and defends

wisdom: knowledge that is gained from having many experiences in life

PANDA

PLAY

What is your favorite way to play?

DOLPHIN

Friendship

Who is your best friend?

ELEPHANT

Wisdom

Do you know someone wise?

HONEY BADGER

Bravery

When can you be brave?

CLOWNFISH
AND
SEA ANEMONE

Harmony

Whom can you live in harmony with?

OWL

Patience

How can you show patience?

WOLF

Loyalty

Whom are you loyal to?

Gentleness

How can you be gentle?

TIGER

Independence

What can you do on your own?

SLOTH

Peace

What makes you feel peaceful?

POLAR BEAR

Love

How do you show love?

PENGUIN

Adventure

What will be your next adventure?